Copyright © 2022 by Jen (Jennifer) Hall

All rights reserved.

No part of this book may be reproduced, restored in a retrieval system or transmitted by means electronic, mechanical, photocopying, recording or otherwise, in any manner, whatsoever, without the written permission of the author. Except in the case of brief quotations embodied in critical articles or reviews.

Poetry by **Jen Hall**
Photography by **Jen Hall**
Cover photo by **Jen Hall**
Book design by **JellyfishCreative.com.au**
Published by **KISS Principle Clontarf Australia**
KISSPrinciple.com.au

ISBN: **978 0 9807222 1 5**

*Tread lightly
Each footprint leaves an impression in my heart*

*Tread kindly
Each footprint takes my breath away*

*The tiniest of feet that tiptoe into my world
tattoo indelible footprints of love in my heart...*

I am grateful

Footprints

2	Prologue
9	My why
17	My mythology
21	A prayer in the darkness
22	Alphabet soup
25	Buddha within Christ without
26	Ambivalence
29	Anniversary
39	Another Mother's Day
41	Beautiful moon
45	Believing is seeing
47	Centred
48	Body as art
51	Butterflies
53	Choice
54	Christina
57	Cityscapes
61	Courageous heart
62	Dark places
65	Death
67	Dear Denise
69	My disenfranchised angel
71	Empty
72	Emily Rose
78	Equality and diversity
81	Estranged birthdays
82	Express yourself
85	Focus
86	FOMO
89	Good enough
90	Gratitude in defeat

Footprints

92	Heart-centred
95	Hero's journey
97	My heart's got this
99	Hello old friend
103	Heart salve
105	It's Christmas again
108	It's not that easy
111	Journey back into the future
114	Linen and silk
117	Breathe
118	Magic
121	Mary, Mary
122	Mother and son
125	Artistry of music
127	Mum and dad
131	Mum's panic
133	My patch
137	Nigel
141	Not sure
142	Only human
148	Opportunity
149	Plasticine
151	Questioning for answers
152	Random hellos
153	Heart centred goals
154	A mother's love
157	"Don't know" mind
158	Mother's Day reflection
159	Defining love
160	There is no I - Only All
163	Remnants of abuse
165	Running screaming towards the light

Footprints

168	Pot of gold
171	Scorpio sister
172	Seven
173	Siblings
177	Simply, sorry
178	Slow dancing with Venus backwards
181	Solidarity sister
184	Spirit of a healing flower
187	Such a pain
188	Sun shower
191	Taking it all in
193	Tears of remorse
195	The wetlands
196	The writing's on the wall
199	Thomas Conor
206	Two Years
211	Unlimited friendliness
215	Walking in the rain
219	War of worlds
222	What am I doing?
225	What if...
226	Where soul meets spirit
229	Why
231	Wishing for peace
232	Wired to survive
234	WTF?!?!
237	Wyzdom
238	Grandmotherhood
241	Milo William
245	Prayer for healing
247	Footprints in my heart
248	Epilogue

My why

My writing has themes which have bubbled to the surface of awareness, as I reflect on what I've written over many years, and how it makes me feel. Writing has been about a journey through love, loss, grief, fear, sometimes even humour, connecting in many ways with something bigger than myself, and rising to love life again.

I have recognised along the way that loss is inherent in life: where I or anyone, perceive gain (a personal attachment to anything), the potential of loss is held constant. Loss and gain can also connect us deeply with the existential crisis of uncertainty. We appear to live in a very anxious world where so many day to day things feel like a threat to our very existence, along with real and present, personal and global dangers. The loss of a sense of security comes with any level of uncertainty. I have come to realise in supporting many clients of all ages, as well as navigating my own ups and downs, that our human potential is to find ways to learn and grow in love within our naturally poignant experience.

Our measure of loss and grief is equal to our capacity to love.

Our capacity to love is perhaps paradoxically, where healing the impact of difficulties begins.

My sense of mine, and other peoples, many losses has been overwhelming at times, and felt in many areas of life. The losses have been actual, physical, symbolic, and at times debilitating to the point where I have wondered if I will go on: at times I've felt uncertain about having a future at all. I'm not alone in that feeling of loss, grief and uncertainty. Like most of us, I do find ways to go on and eventually I do find joy in life again. It's natural that we return to reflect on the deeply felt moments from time to time. I feel blessed and grateful to continue to learn from philosophy, psychology, art, science, spiritual teachings from many cultures, from beautiful human connections, and all coming together with common themes of love, compassion, and kindness as the most powerful basic feelings that can generate the greatest respect for all of life.

I spend much of my life listening to stories of all kinds of loss, struggles, and the impact on lives when people experience everything, from trying to navigate day to day difficulties, to the worst case scenarios you could possibly imagine.

Woven into these writings I hold not only my experiences, but also many memories of conversations with other people and their struggles and resilience, which comes alive in the writing. We are never alone in our experiences even though it may feel like it. As I write about these dark nights of many people's souls, in a way I am trying to normalise, not minimise, the depth of feelings people have shared with me, and then hopefully in many cases I demonstrate not only where we can all feel stuck, but also the possibility of resilience and healing in recognising there can be light at the end of the tunnel.

My hope is that you will experience the metaphorical "death of the author", as you feel your heart resonate with the writing and connect with your own challenges, and your ability to heal from the light of love shining within your own heart.

We can do more than survive, we can thrive.

My own healing focus of deliberately choosing simple thoughts or mantras such as "this too shall pass", the Serenity Prayer, and simply coming back to an enquiry of "is this love?" are great ways to build a resilience muscle and courage in the navigation of life as it presents in all its glory. Simple but not easy...

The well-known short verse from the Serenity Prayer:
"Grant me the serenity to accept the things I cannot change; courage to change the things I can; and wisdom to know the difference."

There can be a resurfacing from the depth of the suffocating, emotional ocean to a breath of fresh air when we surface on a clear still moment of pausing within these thoughts.

I have written about my reflections of grief acknowledged and unacknowledged, grief past and present, grief disenfranchised and anticipatory. I have written about sadness, anger, fear, regret, vulnerability: in mind, body, and spirit. Most of all, may you notice that I have written about love and appreciation for the moments of joy, the depth of experience, and heartfelt connection to something much bigger than myself. When I feel like I've lost my way, and I expect this will happen again, this is my road map back to the present, and a sense that I can go on again. In true Scorpio style, like a Phoenix, I rise from the ashes to continue growing and loving, doing the best I can.

I feel certain we all have this capacity to go through the fire and, like a forest over time regenerate, emerge renewed with new knowledge and skills: an evolutionary and revolutionary process. The key may be to understand and choose carefully which seeds you would choose to water as you regenerate. I, like many people, have found spending time in nature in any way I can inspires me to shift my focus to what is real and present in the moment.

Overtime I have noticed heart shapes everywhere: some created obviously by human hands, and others, nature's own artistry. I find such joy in noticing these hearts everywhere. As you'll see in the following pages I capture images of these hearts. When I see a heart, especially one that nature has sculpted, it takes my breath away and brings me back to awareness of the present moment. Seeing a heart reminds me to reflect on universal love, and with gently inquiry, ask where love is in this moment.

The Wheel of Success© I created in 2009 as a therapeutic tool, is something that helps me to align with my values and remember what will help me grow. The simplicity of unconditional love is where I always come back to when I want to feel centred in the hub of the wheel, centred in life. I, like most people, have times where challenges arise, difficult emotions and experiences confront me, and I step out of love in to an expression of something that is not love, usually fear based. There's been a lot of that around globally for a few years now, which has impacted relationships on very intimate levels as well as globally. In some ways if you look you might see where, not only has the challenge exacerbated division and conflict, it has also mitigated conflict in some ways bringing some people closer with a sense of connection and community.

Fear is a natural part of life and an indicator of threat where we may need to protect ourselves, sometimes to survive. Understanding where fear is real and present danger, or imagined from the many stories we or others weave, is key to finding balance and keeping the nature of reality in our consciousness. It's a very tricky balancing act when we have access to so much information, from sources often unknown. Information or knowledge is not necessarily wisdom.

"The longest most difficult road we will travel is the journey from our head to our heart." (Source unknown)

Those who can hold their fears consciously with awareness, understanding and acceptance are more likely to build resilience and connections: all coming from connecting to our hearts. When we are connected to our heart, instead of reacting, we have a greater opportunity to respond to life as best we can: even if there are things out of our control.

As mentioned above thoughts/words help me to connect with experiences and unconditional love in many ways: even love songs designed for everlasting romance can be connected to the broader sense of love of anyone or anything.

I love Celine Dion's lyrics from the song in the movie Titanic:
"You are safe in my heart and the heart will go on".

I have those lyrics placed on a photo of the three most precious people I could ever lose. Just writing this I feel that gripping lump in my throat, an emptiness in my chest, my eyes well up with tears of regret, loss and grief: and most of all I feel connected to the deepest sense of unconditional love. I have learned that while we might never again be together, we will never be apart while I hold them wrapped in a warm blanket of unconditional love in my heart.

Words and song connects me with experiences and feelings. A song, as often mentioned, is poetry in motion, and an often philosophical healing balm. Perhaps one day some of my poems will become song lyrics... But for now these poems are the words I had, even though words were never enough. May the following words help you connect to love and gratitude in your heart...

Love and loss changes us all forever, leaving indelible footprints in the heart. Each of these moments takes our breath away.

My mythology

WHY AM I HERE?

Spirituality...
I brought it with me, my gestalt
A leap of faith to become
Scorpion, eagle, and phoenix
Stepped out of the void
Into the mud
No mud, no lotus
Scorpion and eagle the roadmap to become phoenix.
Meaning making feels natural to me
It flows with each sense, with each breath
With each dream remembered
Everything sensed is alive with memory, imagination, and connection
All timing, synchronistic perfection
Sometimes livid with stained glass perception.
Spirituality is my mystery
Heart centred presence, my goal
Religion my adversary
Paradoxically, St Ignatius, my saintly guide
Forever obvious by my side.
Metaphysics is my science
A quantum leap of possibility

My mythology

Continued

Energy whispers to my soul
Astrology, in part, my psychology
Philosophy an anthology
Connection to creation is my journey
Unconsciously, strategically keeping company
With all those who would be my teachers.
Words, an attempt to express creatively
Music, the rhythm of the universe beating in my heart
Capturing nature images invites me to reflect on sacred geometry
Symmetry and beauty
Colour and hue
Birth and destruction
Order and chaos
The medicine found in the poison
All systemic by design.
Resilience is my restoration
Awareness is my sight
Acceptance is my heart and soul
Gratitude is my chicken soup
Reflected mirrors, my teacher
Responsibility is my road map

At times a monumental weight to bear
Touching reality spurs me into Action
Attraction is my consequence and reward
Abundance often appears to elude me
Polarisation is my punishment
As I grip tightly to the rim of the Wheel of Fortune
Spinning off into illusion.
Love feels like something to solve
Ancestors and angels all winged from above
Accompanying me always
I'm surrounded by guidance and love
I'm too busy and often ignorant
Too much to say for myself
I'm sure they have much to say too
Thoughts and desires leading me to the fray
Away from the overflowing emptiness
The stillness in the void that fosters Faith
And then I come back to the nature of things
The mystery...
Mystery is my mythology.

A prayer in the darkness

POWER OF PRAYER

This work gets darker
As time goes by
I'm losing my way
That's no lie
The light is there somewhere
But right now, not for me
Right now I'm so stuck
In loathsome company
I'm praying right now
That this darkness in me
Is touched by love
And that God will see
My tears, anger, and grief
Need to heal somehow
I need deep relief
I need light right now
I've lit a candle for prayer
Please show me a sign
Let me know you are within me
Powerfully loving, and divine

Alphabet soup

WORDS ARE NEVER ENOUGH

I love words
Although
Words are not enough
And sometimes too much
Words can heal or harm
Words can be nonchalant
Make the mediocre great
Or the great less than average…
Or merely nothing
Words are limiting
Just symbols thrown together
Alphabet soup
Sometimes delightfully delicious
Or not to our taste
Overcooked
Into a congealed mess of language
Words are labels and inferences
Meaning making
Limited in their goal
Creating boundaries
Often unhelpful
And yet wildly useful in expression.
Words speak of opposites
A continuum
Constrained by the middle space.

Alphabet soup

Continued

Love in the universal sense
Contains all
And is the middle place
Neutral by design.
Hate does not oppose
But is inherent in Love
Hates' connection to fear
Fear does not oppose Love
Fear clutches equivocally
The love of life
Inherent in its existential drive.
Words express limitations
Describing that which is
Un-limited.
Un-bounded
In-finite
End-less
Un-conditional
The limitation inherent in expressing
That which is beyond limits...
Words are not enough
Just Alphabet soup.

Buddha within Christ without

TEACHERS OF LOVE

Buddha within Christ without
Of this priority I have no doubt
Sharing light without and within
Is where the truth of love begins
Christ within and Buddha without
Spreading love around and about
Seeing all with compassion and care
The world changes more when
Love is expressed out there
All the great teachers
Say the same thing
Love without and love within
Makes life feel like eternal Spring.

Ambivalence

POLARIZED

Up and down
To and fro
I've no idea
Which way to go
Moment to moment
Sway here and there
In two my mind
My heart will tear.
Back and forth
From day to day
Ambivalence
I'd like to slay
Polarized
Both ways at once
My mind and heart
So hate the dance

Anniversary

We met for the first time dear soul
A year ago today
Walked side by side along the beach
We both had important things to say

Before we met in person
Your kind words showed up bright
When I lost my dear big brother
Your compassion held me tight

We smiled and shared some stories
Walked barefoot in the sand
And then we stopped for coffee
Bushwalking was the next date we planned

It seemed to be a good day
The stars positively aligned
We'd made plans to meet again
Perhaps some great and grand design

From then we often bush walked and talked
We loved coffees and the views
Had picnics on the grass sometimes
My most favourite things to do

The first kiss took me by surprise
At Ewan Maddock Dam
Your eyes met mine with sweet delight
We smiled and then touched hands

Anniversary

Continued

I remember how my heart felt
Each time I looked into your eyes
The gentle strength inside you
Had me knowing you were wise

I told myself to take it slow
My mantra "one date at a time"
But those beautiful eyes...
And your kind heart
Soon had me leave my chant behind

I listened to the way you spoke
Those things behind the words
The respect and care you showed to all
When entering their worlds

The times when you had been hurt
By people close to you
I heard you hold their heart and space
With such an important bigger view

I thought I saw a future
Aware I didn't really know
So I gave love my best shot
To see how far we'd go

I understood your caution
And followed your steady lead

But I also felt courageous enough
To comfort when there was need

So I told you my true feelings
Not needing tit-for-tat
Wanting you to feel safe with me
Not wondering where I'm at

The gentle touch we exchanged at times
Opened my heart wide
Inviting a beautiful soul like you
Into my life, my heart
Was not taken easily in my stride

Those who came before you
Who had no respect for pain
Had left such a blackened imprint
My heart's been soaked in shame

They taught me to be watchful
Alert for hurt renewed
Vigilant for disrespectful
Although I knew that was not you

I saw your deep sad grief
I saw you hide despair
I worried if one day I'd find
You'd given up on life
No longer there

I felt I understood
As much as one could care
Empathy can't be complete
When broken hearted beyond repair

Anniversary

Continued

Grief filled us both with sorrow
In our own separate solo worlds
We shared mostly the superficial
Depth had so much pain to unfurl

Grief seemed to overtake us
And deep hurt got in the way
We didn't seem to trust each other
With all that we could say

My night dreams are something special
They always tell me true
They showed me things about your world
That were hidden from my view

I should have told you of my dreams
I tried but words were lost
I wish that I had known back then
About the awful cost

Then something deeply tragic happened
And trust couldn't see it through
It seems neither of us were heard
Next thing I know
Us became me and you

I don't know why we did it
And hoped each could explain

Anniversary

Continued

But all you said was goodbye
That you don't hold grudges or blame

Those words left me reeling
Feeling your grudge and the blame
Ok it had to end there, but
We should both have had a chance
To understand and explain

Our griefs will still go on dear soul
Grief can feel the strongest foe
A mark of losing something truly loved
People, dreams
And things that must go

This morning when I awoke
Mixed feelings in my heart
One, a wish to see you again
The other
I need to make a new start

We said we were both tenacious
I had to put it to the test
Today's time and date important
Now or never to let it rest

I saw you walk towards me
A rose held in your hand
You expected me to show today
Walking in the sand

But this was my imagination
My innate sense of hope
It's something I too much rely on
A way for me to cope

So to the beach I travelled
To walk along the sand
Searching all the faces
And for a rose in hand

I knew you weren't there with me
So back to my Plan A
To say goodbye to where I'm stuck
To begin anew today

ANZAC day the day before
I took a sprig of Rosemary with me
Symbolic to the core
I cast it in the waves with tears
To remember loving you no more

Now it's done and dusted
I've said goodbye again
Hoping my symbolic gesture
Would help my sadness end

But I guess it's still in process
And it's going to take some time
I need the hope of some new dreams
To occupy my mind

Love must be where it's meant to be
Because that's just the way it is
I miss you deeply in my life
I still see you through my tears

Anniversary

Continued

But most of all my wish for you
Is that your dreams come true
That you revel in the life you have now
Always knowing that
I loved and appreciated you for you

And for all whom I have lost before
My heart's torn open wide
But the deep meaning of that grief for me
Is that true love never subsides

I need to look where I can help
Where I can truly love and serve
A natural part of myself
I don't want to lose my nerve

Each loss connects us with the last
A natural human trait
We're feeling creatures after all
I guess it's natural fate

The task at hand is to renew
To build resilience and real care
The fact we feel says we're alive
Marked hearts renewed to share

Pick myself up, I'm good at that
I'm a Phoenix after all
I rise to meet another day
Not broken I stand tall

The times you held me in your arms
Your gentle eyes that looked with care
I thank you for those special things
That told me then that you were there

But it's now time to let it go
To end the thoughts of we
To let our spirits take new paths
On this poignant anniversary

Anniversaries are one strange beast
Often celebrations of some great "to-do"
But they can change to say the least
To memories of loss that is true

Whilst mostly these words are true to us
Their reach is far and wide
My daughter, sons, and older brother
The loss of them...
I can't let go the tide

Their loss struck deep, and so many more
As your deep loss did for you
These words all pay deepest respect
To love and loss, theirs too

I'm glad that I believe in love
In joy and sadness too
My heart that breaks from many things
Heals, stays open, and renews

To all the anniversaries: children's births
Special milestones, death, and strife
I'm grateful for the love I have
That gift of all this life.

Another Mother's Day

I MISS YOU

The well feels cold and empty
I've nothing more to give
Some days so dark I wonder
About the will to live
Exhausted beyond measure
It's that kind of day
Mother's Day is nearly over
There's nothing more to say
Not an ounce of joy left in me
As I sit here alone and grieve
My heart so defeated
Unable to wear it on my sleeve
Today life's sweet blessing for me
Was to show that I care
To celebrate my own dear mum
Grateful that she was still there
Too much angst going down

Another Mother's Day

Continued

In my family, my world
I'm so damn tired of it all
All our relationships soiled
The sweet memories of times long passed
Where Mother's Day joy filled our heart
Are treasured little footprints
Even though we're torn apart
Now time to switch off for today
Tomorrow?
Who knows what will come
I'll just keep marking time for now
Until you acknowledge me, your mum
And all the while I realise
That time may never come
To my grave I might grieve
My heart broken open
Never numb

Beautiful moon

Rising full and robust
A beautiful full moon
Low on the horizon
A glowing orange balloon

Above the lapping waves
That are tickling the beach
You capture my heart
 So far out of reach

I can't seem to capture you
Amazed I just stare
My eyes and heart open
Sees your beauty so fair

But the camera lens lies
And I trust what I sense
My eyes don't betray you
With my own minds' eye lens

Mesmerised each night
Full, quarter, or new
My constant sky search
Vigilant for a view

Beautiful moon

Continued

Your power moves oceans
From so far above
Your presence romantic
For those seeking love

Timeless and ageless
You rise like the sun
Some worship in festivals
With dancing and fun

Your rhythm and cycles
We watch and take care
We plant, nurture, and harvest
From your presence up there

We thank you dear moon
And the man up there with you
For eons of interest
Myths, legends, and tides too

Believing is seeing

BELIEVE

Sight is precious, practical, treacherous, and misleading

Taken for granted as we love or hate our world

We read, define, label, judge, enjoy, delight, dismiss

And so much more, all that we see

We know colour, form, faces, familiarities, and strangeness...

The weather forecast by looking at the sky

Rose coloured lenses soften

Like stained glass

Or dirt smeared windows obscure.

For most of us perception is influenced through the lens of memories

Our history

Our DNA

Our filters

We map out our joys and sorrows, fears and love.

Believing is seeing

Continued

At times we can't see through the dense fog of our mind

Internal weather of sunshine and storms

Clouding our vision

Not seeing the beauty and truth of what stands before us

But we are still looking none the less.

And then there is in-sight, the vision of the source of creation, of intuition

With beautiful windows to the spirit, the soul

Insight on a clear day is seeing with our heart

The organ that sees beauty, truth, perfection, faith

In all that might be imperfect to our external perception

Insight sees 360 degrees.

Eyes with fallible lenses see with blinkers and blinders

When sight is lost, heart is open, insight steps up to the plate

A new multidimensional view of life.

Centered

No credit

No blame

No loss

No gain

No black

No white

No polarity

In-sight

Body as art

EYE OF THE BEHOLDER

My body

A living work of art

All colours shades and hues

Textures grains and weaves

Fabric of reality

Structure soft round bony

Sculpted inside and out.

In the eye of the beholder

Likes and dislikes

Moods captured

Light and dark

Ever changing

Pain and joy

Disowned resigned and accepted

Who is the artist?

Butterflies

INSPIRED BY MARK NEPO

There are butterflies today
Flitting here and there catching the light and the breeze
Safe from the cyclonic wind gusts, in the sanctuary of the tree walled garden
Lilly Pillies at full stature ready to bloom
And Kauris, even taller majestically reaching up to the sky.
I am sad, lost in another time and place
And the world is still sacred and beautiful...
Everyday.
Butterflies, buttercup gold, red-white-black
Chocolate brown dancing with bright indigo
Some are as blue as the sky on clear days
Or white wings lightly edged in black, as if gently dipped in the night sky
Floating and flitting around the gently swaying blossoms and leaves
Flapping gently close enough to my lips to kiss
Feeling the breath of their pulsing wings as they seek my attention
The heartbeat of the world speaking to me, wordlessly.
There are butterflies today
Movement so close catching my eye
Reminding me there is always beauty
Butterflies aerial dance leads my eyes

Butterflies

Continued

To the iridescence of lush green grass
Shimmering leaves sparkling as if gold
As the tallest trees sway and bend to the will of the wind
Their movement catching the light and warmth of the sun
Beckoning all to its light
The flowers blossoming
Inviting all to rejoice in their hues, fragrance, and nectar
All creatures crawling, stalking, flying on the wind
Self-actualizing uniquely.
There were butterflies today
Reminding me in the sadness they were there…
Reminding me of beauty
Expanding my vision
Inside and out
Reminding me my heart can hold all things with equanimity and grace
A renewed smile in my heart
Faith in the order of things.
Thank you
Again
You took my breath away…

Choice

What I choose in this moment

Creates the next experience

Becomes this moment

I choose and create, perpetually.

This is my life.

I create it!

Christina

FRIENDSHIP

To my dear friend I'm so grateful to know
In your grounded presence I see your courageous heart glow
You've got many great years ahead my friend
I see a role model towards which, other people's ways bend
Your keen sense of justice and confidence bright
Strengthens confidence in others to show up right
You've been my guiding star for many years
Us sitting together through trials and tears
We've laughed and prayed along the way
Shared simple things from day to day
All treasured moments to be sure
My wish is that there will be many more
I celebrate you today and everyday
Your smiles, your strength and courage,
All your unique ways
You've taught me much about friendship and care
The special ways you've always been there
Your presence in people's lives is clear
Generous in kindness and love, holding all so dear
You deserve such magic and joy to behold
I wish for you that your dreams all unfold.

Cityscapes

PROTECT OUR WORLD

Cityscapes
Concrete drapes
Splash of green
Almost unseen
Twisted wire
Artistic fire
Traffic noise
Lacks any poise
Smog we breathe
Without reprieve
Trees in this place
Will offer Grace
Save the flowers
Don't build more towers
Please appreciate

Cityscapes

Continued

Nature's fate
It's in the hand
Of councils grand
Let's hope they think
Of future's brink
Nothing left
No future bequest
Let's sow right seeds
Nature pleads
Care for our Earth
Let's create rebirth.

Courageous heart

COURAGE

It takes courage

Strong shoulders to bare the load

Soft hands to gently hold life

A bold heart

Open and inherently wise

Nimble fingers guided by love

Gently peeling the onion

Layer by Layer

Stinging our sensitivity

Eyes blinking through tears

Seeking clearer vision

Tears washing away the suffering

Just enough to soothe the broken soul

Without erasing why

We found our courageous heart

Dark places

FACING THE SHADOW

Dark Places
Hollow faces
Holy cow
I'm back there now
Trust dissolving
I'm de-evolving
Human nature
Diminishing stature
A darkened heart
Tears apart
Til nothing's left
A soul bereft
Where's the light
Shining bright
A true heart smile
That won't defile
A lifelong dream
So far unseen
Horrid reflection....
No more rejection
Please.....

Death

INSPIRED BY THICH NHAT HANH

Oh my God

You've gone to the light

No more are you suffering

But now out of sight

I'll miss you so much

But I'll know that you're near

Your quirky signs

And symbols clear.

Say hi in my dreams

I welcome you there

I can see you more clearly

Your bright smile and your hair

Your unique signs of you

Death

Continued

Are the treasures we know

They'll show us your presence

Even after you go.

You've simply transformed

As all energy does

Think of water, clouds, and rain

And that cycle of unconditional love

You see

You are the water and soil

And even a cloud

New seeds will spring from you

Your energy always proud.

Dear Denise

DREAMS

He stands in the light behind you

His hands gently on your shoulders

Blue suit smart and resplendent

He's smiling now

Knowing he will not grow older.

He wants you to know

He will always be there

Walking gently beside you

With tenderness and care.

My disenfranchised angel

For Daniel and all the disenfranchised angels...

MY BEAUTIFUL SON DANIEL 9TH AUGUST 2001

I dreamed a dream, so big I dared
I longed for another child this family's love could share

A sister and brother to welcome you with love
I dreamed so fervently for the gift of you from heaven above

You did all the right things expected of you sweet child
Signs of your presence were there, although the feelings were gentle and mild

Other happenings within me signalled that things were not right
Things went astray, you got stuck my dear boy, and I got a hell of a fright!

I was convinced you were with me, I spoke to your heart
You replied "I'll be back", giving me quite a start

I didn't know the meaning of those words loud and clear
Until I lost your sweet life in that very sad year

They didn't believe your existence, told me to "go get a life"
And then we saw your tiny beating heart, and the signs there was strife

They don't understand how I can feel such great loss and grief
For a heartbeat, a voice, and my little boy's life so brief

My disenfranchised angel

Continued

Your grandmother, and mine, together helped you go to the light
Bringing you to me daily so I could see that you were alright

I awoke from a nap when you would have been eleven
I knew the instant you woke me, you were with me from heaven

Sensing little fingertips on my eyelids, your feather-light healing touch
You were caring for my eyes, and I thank you so much

At times I can sense you. You visit my dreams in the night
Your presence is welcome always, your love, and your light

I've seen you keep company with your family you never met
In my dreams, your brother and sister's good company you've kept

I wish I could have saved you and held you near to my heart
It's some other big plan that had us drawn far apart

So my angel they may discount you, and disenfranchise our love
But I know you are with me from heaven above...

Empty

It feels hopeless

But I go on

Life feels helpless

And it goes on

I feel empty

Just as it should be

An empty vessel

Waiting for love to fill me

I am my own healing

I am grateful

Emily Rose

MY BEAUTIFUL DAUGHTER - YOU TOOK MY BREATH AWAY

Today is such a special day
Each year it comes around
This year you equal 31
And my joy knows no bounds

From just a twinkle in our eyes
Some hurdles got in the way
And then eventually the joy of knowing
In about 9 months would be your special day

I say you are a miracle
Told I would never have
Determined you were right from the start
To meet your mum and dad

The eighth of the eighth, eighty eight
A most auspicious day
A beginning of the highlight
You formed with some delay

The doctors told us no
You really were not there
And to our delighted surprise
Your fieriness was clear

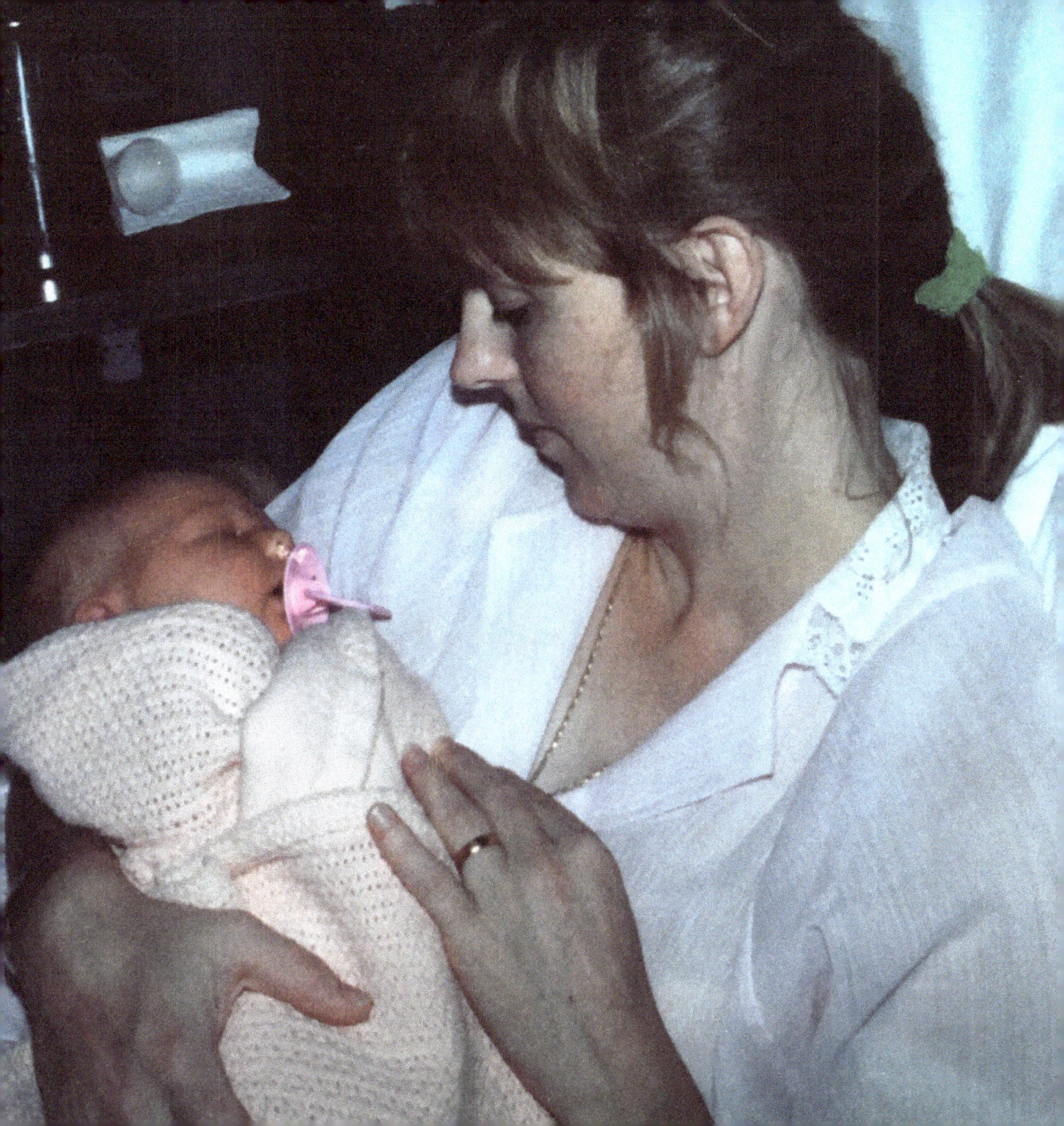

Emily Rose

Continued

Your aunt nicknamed you "Coco"
The size of a coco bean
The blessing of each ultrasound
Your heartbeat could be seen

I fell in love with you Emily Rose
When I knew that you were there
Your presence in my tummy
A blessing more than my dreams dared

To feel the first sweet flutter
And feel my body grow
Helped me believe my dream came true
A dream that you should know

First some flutters and then the kicks
And then hiccups did delight
All movement in my tummy
Letting me know that you were alright

As I felt my body changing
A sure sign that you were there
Once morning sickness ended
I didn't have a care

I just loved every minute
The chilli cravings and short soup too
Just feeling you alive and growing
...My pregnancy with you

I used to hug your dad real tight
So he could feel you move
The kicking and the hiccups
Had him share the joy too

On the day of your birth
Your dad and I were there
We went through it together
So you'd know that we both care

Is it Emily Rose or Prudence?
I'm sure we named you right
Your Rose-Red nickname grew on you
Your red hair outa sight

It was such a joy to watch you blossom
As one day you will know for sure
To see your child develop and grow
Just makes you love even more

Emily Rose

Continued

Reading books, and singing songs to you
Brought a smile to your face
And you became a singer
Your beautiful voice like angels grace

Whilst I didn't get it right it seems
Motherhood felt like I was blessed
I was enchanted by your presence
Even though it looks like I made a mess

Through hardest choices that I've made
I've missed so much about your life
I'll always have such deep regret
And gratitude in how you've thrived.

Now many years have passed since the day
When they said "Hey, you have a girl"
But I can still smell sweet baby hugs
And I remember your gorgeous red curls

There's not much I can give you now
Your happiness is my prayer
The love and care I hold for you
In my heart, will always be there

You just need to think it
And you'll know in your heart
That while we're not together
Mums and their kids are never apart.

And so today I count my blessings
And I thank god above
For this precious gift I was given
This girl that I so love

Happy birthday dearest Em
May all your dreams come true
May you enjoy the deepest blessings
That true love can bring to you.

Equality and diversity

Tormented by equality and diversity

Equal rights

Equal opportunity

Equal pay

Equal acceptance

Equal compassion

Equal attention

Equal love...

Egalitarian parenting...

How does a parent ensure children feel equally loved?

Equality starts at home

Charity begins at home

Grace gravitates from the home

Faith flourishes from the home

Home is where the heart is...

Sadly,

We don't always get it right.

Estranged birthdays

I MISS YOU

It's your birthday again today and still we are apart

The heaviness and joy I feel rips open wide my heart

For more than half your life you've pushed away my presence

I'm so sorry that what we've been through has you unable to see my essence

As always I wish you all the best, I wish you joy and love and all

And I hope with all my might that we reunite before I fall

One day we'll both be gone my love, I know that then we'll reunite

But let's work at peace and love right now to end this soul destroying fight

I've watched my family fall apart and wonder why it's so

What's the journey meant to be? Perhaps I'll never know

But not knowing doesn't stop me from a hopeful desire for us to heal

True magic is for us all to sit together, share stories, and a meal

I'd love to hear your stories about your life and how it goes

I want to see if, just like at birth, you have ten fingers and ten toes

I miss you every single day... we're wasting so much time

But I hold you safely in my heart, my true love for you is divine.

Express yourself

CREATIVITY HEALS

Express yourself

Be creative

Whatever that means

Add a spoonful of love

A sprinkle of stardust

Overflow a cup of faith

Stir it with joy

Allow to germinate ferment and grow

Bake and enjoy

Consume and nourish

Heart and soul

Dance

Smile…

Focus

When we focus on our back yard

our back yard is all we will see.

Focus on the Universe

then there is opportunity to see every possibility.

FOMO

LOVE AND LOSS

I'm most likely going to die

With ruptures unrepaired

My regrets always held close

Un-forgiveness I've despaired

I'm not alone in this fear

It's an existential trial

To solve this tragedy of the heart

Means to go the extra mile

FOMO is for me

Not missing out on pleasure

Instead, missing out, my sorrys not received

I feel pain of sadness beyond measure

I fear FOMO for you too my loves

Knowing the deep pain of regret

There comes a time of "too late"

Wishing for you

When that time comes

Not to fret

Yes I have FOMO

Of the superficial in life

But the most fearful anticipation

Is the result of heart strife

The cost of relationships

That break open wide

Is the stuff grief is made of

A deep and strong flowing tide.

Good enough

PERSPECTIVE

Am I good enough?
A question I hear many ask daily
A question I see many struggle with
Sometimes not even questioned
Simply believed
"I'm not good enough!"
It's more common that you think.
Where does this idea arise?

Before conscious thoughts and words
Innocence just watches, learns, smiles, plays
Sometimes tears seek empathy and care
Looking into a mirror of feelings
Dependent on the smile to be reflected in kindness
And on care with compassion to help us feel whole.

But ah ha! So we see "I'm not good enough"
When other looks back telling a different story
A soulful expression of someone else's pain
A frown or scowl projecting
Anger, impatience, or disappointment
Care is not forthcoming in simple times of need
They don't feel good enough, and so
Projecting their pain onto a blank canvas
Just waiting to be coloured by the palette of life.

Gratitude in defeat

SURRENDER

Eyes closed in prayer

Wishing so deeply

That healing was there

Shoulders drooped so low

Softened completely

With nowhere to go

Moist eyes and tears soften my skin

Tears sting my cheeks no more

Toxins removed

Just droplets of love

Like waves to the shore

There's nowhere else to go now

Except to sink deeply within

Aversion and anger dissipate

With my wish to renew and begin

With the peace and compassion

On the wings of a white dove

Sadness, the ripened fruit

From the tree of life and love

Its harvest bittersweet

I'm relieved and there's thankfulness

As I sink deeply into defeat

My soul sighs in peace thinking

No more need to defend her

She's letting go into love

And the faith and freedom of surrender

Heart-centred

Look at the world

Through a heart-centred lens

Befriend life

In all her glory

Hero's journey

INSPIRED BY JOSEPH CAMPBELL

A hero's journey

In Joseph's words

Is how we stop

Horrendous turds

From leading us

Along a difficult track

We fight, gain strength

Give life a whack

Laughter's what

I need right now

As I try to soothe

My furrowed brow

Recollecting motherhood

And all its hurts

Hero's journey

Continued

There's no such thing

As just deserts

All that's been

Misunderstood

We've lost connection

A familyhood

Mostly wishing

I could undo time...

Instead I'm stuck

In childish rhyme

How to undo

And erase regret

A question my heart

Will leave unmet.

My heart's got this

This time of year comes as a cluster
Of poignancy that can be felt with all senses
Like dark chocolate, bittersweet new layers added as years pass by
A winter's chill, these months seem to feel frozen in time
Like a cold still lake reflecting life back to be seen in its truth
… going to get through this with as much love as I can muster.
With the courage of holding true to all that I value so highly
With the faith that love can conquer or transcend anything
With the hope for deepest healing soothing all hearts
With trust that all is as it should be
With serenity of divine grace flowing through me
With peace everlasting, is that even possible?
With the gentleness of soft, strong hands lovingly holding me
I will get through this with more generosity of spirit than ever before.
Then comes springtime… and with it the soothing warm light of release
Breathing again then
Until this time next year…

Hello old friend...

A conversation with Autoimmune Disease

INSPIRED BY THICH NHAT HANH

Hello old friend
You're back again
I'm hoping you're not here to stay
Perhaps interfering with how I play
You cause me worry, fear, and grief
Sometimes I feel like you're a thief
When you attack you show no mercy
You've changed my life irreversibly
I'm not the only one you know
You're visits around the world just grow
Old friend your social nature is true
Your visits to us all just grew and grew
I can't pretend that I'm not home
Or just not answer your call to my phone
When I slammed the door hard in your face
You found the backdoor and entered with grace
Whilst I'd prefer that you weren't here

Hello old friend

Continued

Your fiery determination is absolutely clear
I get that your intentions are really well meant
However dear friend your mind is bent
You're so misguided my dear friend
I wish you attacking me would just simply end
Like a hurricane that destroys all in her path
You work too hard leaving a horrible aftermath
Your power hurts bodies in so many ways
Like cancer, but slower, you burn through our days
You're tiring me out, I could sleep through the day
When you force your way in, in your own wicked way
You've visited me often throughout the years
Hurting my body and causing me tears
You're hurting our bones and even stripping sight
Your frenzied attention has too much might
If I fight you as you've done to me before
I know that you'll just break down my door
So if it hurts me more to resist your presence
Then I welcome you, focused on your true essence

I welcome you and acknowledge you're there
Hoping we can work together with care
Instead I'll try a soothing action
So you might feel a kind retraction
What can I do to make you feel more at home
To take away your fire, make you less attack-prone
When doctors and medicine intervene my friend
It's your fiery-ness they're trying to amend
They're not trying to take you right out of the race
Just show you the nature of your true beautiful face
They're not trying to totally bring you down
Just make you see sense to balance your ground
We know your role as protector and care
But your enthusiasm has you fight unaware
Acceptance and compassion feel like the key
For me, us all, and immunity to live in harmony
So I'll do what I can to notice you're here
With a kind open heart and presence so clear
I'll nurture my body and move with care

Hello old friend

Continued

I'll do all I can to help you play fair
I'll show you great warmth to cool your great crime
Hoping you'll notice your real job of fighting the grime
Maybe you'll notice my caring for you
And you'll learn your best manners in our body too
You've slowed down our joy and stomped on our dreams
I've wished you to hell with the worst of means
But I can dream again my friend
I'll find another way to bend
As long as I have something to say
I'll find another way to play
You are my body and I love you
I hope one day that you'll love me too.

Heart salve

PRESENCE

The scent of honey wafting by me on the gentle breeze
Dragonflies with their aerial antics, flies buzzing
And of course then there's the humming bees
Pollinating nature, busily calm in their daily fulfilment of duty
In my presence, I wonder if they understand
How their natural community creates such beauty
Magnificent butterfly wings swing past in a flash moment to behold
Birdsong, the softest twittering
Kookaburras laughing, and Butcher Bird melodies so bold
The warm glow of morning sunlight on leaves gently tickling the airwaves
Dew on the grass in the cool damp shadows cast by the trees
The fallen leaves, cut grass and earth
Creates a sanctuary for crawling critters with ease
Flowers glowing with natural beauty
As they offer their cheek to the kisses of morning sunlight
All of nature uplifting my world into presence
I see how life can truly be seen, in beauty
Like the smile of a child so innocent and bright
Thank you, you took my breath away, brought my senses alive
Brought a glowing smile to my face
You reawoke me to life with this dance of nature
In my sanctuary filled with grace.

It's Christmas again

Here we go...
Onto the merry-go-round, that roller coaster ride
Emotions all over the place
We slip and we slide
Torn between joy
Whilst gnashed by tearing pain
Each year it comes around and we do it all again.

Missing those loved who are not in our midst
Perhaps now passed away
Present as a spiritual mist.
We drink their good health
May even shed a tear
Remembering times of some far Christmas past
Held on to tight and dear.

And then there's the conflict that makes our heart ache
A chest hard and empty
For love's own sweet sake.
For many, the harshest of times
Driving some to drink
Instead of sharing tea towels and warm talks around the kitchen sink.

It's Christmas again

Continued

We hold such high expectations of sweet Christmas dreams
Sugar plum fairies, love, rainbows...
Hurt makes room for itself it seems.
I'm driven to know how
To build a bridge to your soul
Everyday about kindness and love that never grows old.

Each day, not just Christmas I wish you so much
Sending you air hugs and etheric mail
That miss the warmth of tender touch.
The conflict might heal
Or even might grow ever hot
My heart just stays open, but empty, within a tight painful knot.

The day's nearly over, relief that soon I'll breathe again
Step off the roller coaster
That damned merry-go-round, my sanity to fend.
The conflicts continue
Without even a spoken word...
Silent treatments as sharp as an unscabbarded sword.

It's time to alight this mad, crazy ride
It gets more tiresome each year
As we slip and we slide.
I'm letting you go now
I'm setting all free
Still loving you deeply, while missing your precious company.

The company this Christmas was genuine, kind and true
How blessed I felt feasting with beautiful souls
While still missing you.
All of us were missing
Someone dear in our heart
We all raised our glasses to the dearly departed, or someone worlds apart.

It's not that easy…

LAUGHTER IS MEDICINE

It's just not that easy
I wish it were
To work through things
That cause despair

The nature of
Despair itself
Is deep, it's harsh
Beyond natural health

It washes through
A tsunami type flood
Soaking heart and mind
As if with red blood

It crushes souls
Defeats all hope
Taking away
Any semblance to cope

One day we'll be gone
And it won't matter then
So be kind to self always
With sanity to fend

It's good to remember
This too shall pass
And focus on gratitude
Not fall on your arse 🙂

Journey back into the future

My beautiful bouncing baby girl
I dreamed of you one night
The dream showed you as older
I awoke with such a fright
I dreamed you were just three years old
All dressed in purist white
You were laying in a coffin
A heartbreaking deathly sight
Eye closed, shut tight
Long red curls framed your innocent face
Deathly pale, your life had failed
No sign of life could be traced.
I didn't know the meaning then
Just felt such deep, sad grief
Awoken now, holding my baby tight
The dream had been a thief.
I reflect back often about that dream

Journey back into the future

Continued

I look how things became
A fiery girl at three years old
To match your curly red mane.
Things changed for ever then it seemed
Don't think of it as right or wrong
Just you becoming your own true self
Singing your own unique song.

At three you held a tea party
Feeding Somalia's starving children, you said
Already advocating for the innocent
As if your innocence was dead.
Your fiery nature blossomed then
At three you showed some fight
Independent and taking charge
We felt your courage and fiery might.
Now you fight for justice

Political causes dear to your heart
Looking back...
The coffin was a symbol
Of transformation, a new start.
You standing for equality
Lights up where justice ends
Your fiery heart for others
Stands tall to make amends.
I wish in ways it had been different
That together we had walked the path to now
But perhaps it's a much grander plan
Important to the world somehow.
Take notice of your dreams my child
At times they portend of things to come
Insight could have been a blessing back then
Perhaps preventative medicine...
Between a daughter and her mum.

Linen and silk

Luxury is my bed at night
The tactile joy of crisp linen sheets
The scent of sunshine in the weave
All delighted senses my bed meets

The silken doona as soft as down
The pillows puffed up with might
The soft white rug… words of course, the decor
"Home, Life, Enjoy, Love," … The feeling is just right

At night when I climb Mt Everest into my bed
My body exhausted at best
I snuggle into my bed's arms sweet delight
Comforting, and inviting me to rest

I feel my face crack wide open with smiles
Thought I was beyond too tired to do
The joy of this warm, safe, friendly space
Rouses giggles just like a child would do

Pure & Simp
Sweet Love
Sweet Home
Living
Sweet
Love
For the Pure &
Enjoy Your Life
Sweet
Home
Enjoy Your Life

Linen and silk

Continued

As I drift into dreams and sleep's sweet repose
I greet joy and a tranquil mood
My body softly floats away on a cloud
Melting like warm chocolate into deepest gratitude

When I rouse from sweet dreams taking time to reflect
On these wonderful chilled winter mornings
Silk and linen beckon me to stay
The space still so cosy and warming

So coffee is brewed, poured into my favourite old mug
With crema and froth of warm winter milk
Then back to sweet comfort and deep gratitude
Delighting in the luxury
Warm crisp linen, and soft cosy silk...

Breathe

MEDITATION

Breathe the eyes into friendliness

Breathe the face into a welcoming smile

Breathe the heart into openness

Breathe consciously as if all our lives depend on it

Breathe to soften the world into Grace

Magic

Magic is not the illusions we perceive

Magic is the truth we experience and understand

From a stance of love and gratitude.

Mary, Mary

FRIENDSHIP

Mary, Mary, not contrary
How does your garden grow?
With Faerie folk, angels, spirits, and love
And oracle cards all in a row

Mary, Mary, you step through life
Meeting it all head on
With fears to face you show courage and grace
And show all that you are strong

Mary, Mary, you take such care
Counselling young who are facing their foe.
Your kind words and encouraging skill
Your empathy helping kids to grow.

Mary Mary not contrary
I'm glad to call you my friend
May you embrace life's good grace
And celebrate without end.

Mother and son

MANON AND NIC

Kindness and care is all that I see
Walking hand in hand a mother and son
Keeping great company
A loving son supportive and true
Showing his mum he is there for her too
My heart opened wide, a lens finding this treasure
As I captured a moment of love beyond measure
A bond for a lifetime I see you both there
A true love connection of gratitude kindness and care.

Mother:
You inspire this bond so proud of both sons
They've learned from their mum
From your love, they have won.

Son:
I see your true heart of a man who can hold
All that life has to offer
Your loving heart, truly bold.

Artistry of music

AILEEN

Our heart attunes to the magical tones of music through our ears and nerves

The lyrics of songs are poetry in motion that speak to our hearts through our mind

Evoking and invoking

The tempo of music speaks to our beating heart through rhythm and time

Shared music with others resonating with hearts attuned

Synchronises to the heartbeat of community spirit

Listen deeply with your heart

Seek your own heart-song as you sing along with life

Dance to your own heartbeat and the rhythm of your soul

Moment to moment find joy in music

Reawaken to life

Mum and dad with love

VIETNAM

You gave me life, love, and care
In your own unique way
Shaped by the way that you were raised
Ancestry always guides the way

You took us to places exotic and strange
Something so special in those times
We saw amazing cultures, people, and faiths
A unique treat to our young minds

Dad you left to go fight a war
And mum you were left to hold the fort
Back in those days these things were done
Without any help, guidance, or support

I don't know how you did it
Overtime the impact is seen
You both suffering the consequences
A continued inner war unseen

Mum and dad with love

Continued

It makes you both my heroes
As I try to understand
The trials and tribulations
You both have been dealt in this difficult hand.

Parents don't get a handbook
I've found how hard it can be
To raise happy children who know they are loved
Whilst keeping some sense of sanity

Something being a parent gave to me
Besides the love I feel for my own kids
Was to understand with all my heart
That, like us all, the best you could
Is what you both did

You raised us all to leave the nest
And it was our turn to find our way
You've always welcomed us back with open arms
And supported when things went astray

We've only ever had to ask
And sometimes you simply gave
Your home, your love, and even funds
In fact, of anything you have

I write this poem with love and care
And know things can be pretty rough
Aging can be such a bitch
And I see you both doing it tough

I'm here for you as you have been
Here for us all through strife
I'll walk beside you all the way
Through this difficult journey of life

So where ever I wander in this big world
Let's keep close with love in our hearts
As I've learned with my kids in the most powerful ways
Even if we can't be together
We're never really apart.

Mum's panic

EQUALITY IN LOVE

Today I feel a panic as
I publish words, I fear
That never will be read
By those that I hold dear
My panic is my children
Who fill me with such love
Will not believe that they are equally
Held in my heart with love
I wrote for you dear Emily
A note of birthday care
To let you know deep in my heart
You'll always be there
But Tom I felt this panic
Worried you would feel left out
You wondering if I love you too
And I want to leave no doubt
I thought "what if something happens"
Before I get the chance
To write you a birthday note

Mum's panic

Continued

Events could take it out of my hands
I worried you'd never hear me say
The specialness that's you
As I have worried throughout parenting
Equally for both of you.
I know that you are different souls
Each equal in unique ways
Both deserving everything good
Each and every day
Today as I reflected on you both
I hold each with equal care
If I never get to say it to your face
Or hug you with so much love to share
So I'd like to stop this panic now
Of trying to be fair
I love you both equally
Similarities and differences,
All to be loved, and to show you that I care.

My patch

I love where I live

Hearts abound

Everywhere I look

There's joy to be found

Nature's artist paints hearts

In the grass and the trees

The beauty of the ocean

The touch of see breeze

The birds swooping deep

Dive into blue green

Fish glide gracefully around my feet

Thinking they are unseen

A billion trillion diamonds

Sparkling on the ocean

My patch

Continued

Kayak bobbing up and down

The bay in gentle motion

To walk cycle or paddle

And just gaze at it all

Fills my heart with gladness

And gratitude for all

I treasure the friendships

Of people close by

We reflect over coffee

We hug laugh and cry

We debate the state of the world

And share family tales too

We all love where we live

Our gratitude is true blue.

SHELL HEART BY PAUL MONDIENTZ

Nigel

FRIENDSHIP

Once I wrote poem
About how words are not enough
To describe important things
Finding the best words can be tough.
To use words to capture feelings
Of who you are to me
Would limit something special
About a friendship 'tween I and Thee.
But I want to have a go my friend
Because words are all I have
To tell you what you mean to me
About friendship, gratitude, and love.
It's been about 39 years now
Months, give or take a few
When we first "disco'd" out in Canberra
And shared a bevvy or two.
A friendship soon developed
We shared a house with fun

Nigel

Continued

Getting into all kinds of mischief
And long gardening sessions in the sun.
We all loved the tuna casserole
Although no one loved to clean the dish
A blue-green science experiment developed
As we all hope another cleaned it....what a wish!
We partied pretty hard sometimes
Somethings still remain a blur
But many things remain so clear
Of memories that we share.
Your cuddles and care when I was sick
Our laughter and loads of fun
Our spiritual stuff we had in common
Great memories second to none.
Us working in the salon
Playing artists of design
And you my friend, your creative soul
Your amazing skill leaves most of us behind.

You were there at special moments

In all my joy you did delight

Building snowmen with us in Dublin

Playing board games into the night.

Your depth of soul so wise at times

Takes my breath away

The creative way you show the world what's important,

Through a magical sense of play.

Your depth and joyful sense of fun

Expressed when you create and write

Provokes deepest belly laughter

As we understand your deeper message

And meaningful great insight.

Your optimism that rides the waves

Of life's ups and downs and strife

Inspires many, including me

To step with confidence and care through life.

So my friend this mindful poem reflects

Nigel

Continued

On the joy of seeing you
Alive and well and making the most
Of everything you do.
It's heart-warming to see you loved and in love
An amazing husband by your side
I see you both filled with love and light
As you both roll along with the ebb and flow of the tide.
I wish for you continued love
And joy in all you do
I'm blessed to have these 39 years
Of friendship and love with you.
May there be many more…

Not sure

Not really sure what I am doing
Not really sure how I feel
The pendulum turning circles
Not sure if I have healed.

Wildness rises within me
Passion comes to the fore
This time it rises for me
I deeply desire so much more.

My soul is chasing my heart
Logic chasing around in my mind
Navigating doubt, and uncertainty whilst
Hoping new direction I'll find.

I'm definitely not feeling fearless
But courage has risen for sure
To risk new adventures I'd love to try
My wildness wanting to know more.

What is love anyway?
I'm not sure that any of us knows
We're continually trying to define it
An unanswerable question I suppose.

Only human

WE THINK WE KNOW

I see my value
No greater or less than all living beings
And maybe the inanimate too
Just a thing
With human traits and frailties
I reflect on my errors
My impact on other beings
Their impact on me.
I think of attraction of things and people
I think about what angers me
What presses my injustice button
Most of all right now…
The selling out of spirituality
The monetisation of knowledge and wisdom
The attempted ownership of power inherent in all things.
It comes down to simple things
A KISS principle
We make it more complex
We try to imitate systems within a chaotic world

Only human

Continued

Thinking that we know
Or even know better than the chaos.
We can't avoid
Only endure it all
Move through
All that could be neutral by design.
We look through human eyes
We seek through human desires
We interpret the material and physical world
Through human perception.
Even philosophy disagrees
Reinvents itself
All based on observations through human lenses
As unique as DNA.
We learn and teach with human limitations
Saying we are unlimited
Forgetting we are flesh as well as energy.
We seem to think we know
How to defeat suffering

Does suffering really exist?
It's such a personal experience.
We experience disease, happiness, famine, war,
Love, good health, joy, loss...
What of the trees in the forest?
What do trees "think"?
How do they perceive suffering if it exists
A fungus destroys
Pestilence devours
Does the tree suffer?
Did it attract the experience?
I wonder if the tree knows its purpose
Uniquely and collectively
All answerable by human projection.
We are simply human
Albeit with an inexplicable connection to something beyond the self
It's all that we have
Yet we think we know...
We cannot truly know

Only human

Continued

Physically just part of ecology
We are part of the food chain
Both predator and prey
Physical and energy
As with all things manifest
No better or worse
But glorified by ego
We think we know...
The lion has skills to kill to survive
The Gazelle knows to run like the wind
Take away the wolves and see how
Elk change the course of nature
No predator checking their numbers
They change the course of rivers
And so much more
We think we know...
The hunter and hunted eons ago
Became only the predator
An ecosystem prey in our path

All out of balance
Some species lost forever
The natural order of things?
We think we know...

What is intelligence?
What other species harms itself?
Takes its own life?
Microcosmically hurtful to self
Macrocosmically polluting our home
Endangering all that is life.
Animals don't seem to defecate in their own nest
Do they?
We think we know
We don't...
We are animals, that's all
Death transforms back to energy
And then the spiral continues.
We think we know...

Opportunity

In every opportunity there lies an obstacle

And

Within every obstacle lies the seed of opportunity

Look with your heart so the opportunity will arise

To see it all

Then choose wisely

Plasticine

SHAPED BY LIFE

Inanimate
Just a pliable blob
Lifeless
Even useless really
Kind of abstract
In an undefined shape
Until
Somebody touches it
Applies pressure
Moves it in some way
Shapes its reality
It doesn't move itself
Moulded by experience
Not self-directed at all
Just plasticine

Questioning for answers

I wonder what is truly sustainable for me,
I ask for guidance.

What do I need to release
to move forward in service to share any gifts I have?

What do I need to do to balance humility and ego,
so that my actions are an expression of Grace moving through me?

The answers to these questions are my prayer.

May I listen with my heart
and be open to receiving these answers.

Random hellos

Thinking of you makes me smile

From ear to ear, so worthwhile

A greeting to tell you how I may

Wish you love and kindness from day to day.

Heart centred goals

Each step I take towards my heart...
My dreams step closer to me.

A Mother's love

FOR DANIEL, TOM, AND EMILY

Through joyful moments, caring and laughter
And even in the gloom
Through tears, tests, and trials
A mother's love can grow and bloom.

Each child is a celebration
A miracle and a joy
A chance for a mother to learn and grow
A magnificent harvest of the seeds we sow.

Meditating on your special day
Holding my love for you in my heart
It seems we can't be together
And yet
We've never been apart.

"Don't know" mind

PERSPECTIVE

You don't know me
You think you do...
But it's not possible for you to really know me
Do you want to even try to know me
Are you curious about me
Or are you curious about reflections of you within me
Or maybe just you...

I don't know me.
Sometimes I think I know me
But I don't
It's not possible to really know me
Just concepts and constructs of others reflected
Or maybe God.
How curious am I about "I" or "me"...

I don't know you
Sometimes I think I know you, but I'm misinformed
I know of concepts and constructs, projections and paradigms
And if my heart-mind is open I know about lenses
I only know of you through my eyes
And the door of my heart-mind
Is the door closed or open
Even then
I still don't truly know you
Or me...

Mother's Day reflection

My heart is so full that it aches to its core
Love spilling over that transcends time and space, pain and wrongness.
Some hearts may never mend with mind interfering
Those cold harsh memories
Some memories with questionable truth.
But...
When the heart knows no bounds love and life become eternal
Past, present, and future
All wrapped in a warm blanket of love.

I reframe the idea that
Rising like a phoenix means to cut the chains from the past to be free
Free of all history, or that
Erasing memory is the way to rise and be free of history
And so becomes the tipping point for insanity.

Would I want to eliminate history and erase memory?
How would I learn which was love and which was not?
So I say...
To remember which was love and which was not
To rise like a phoenix and embrace the past with love, care, and compassion
For knowing deeply the past, is the tipping point for sanity in the present and future.

Defining love

Infinity

Eternally

A crude measurement

Of the immeasurable...

Love

There is no I – only all

INTERBEING

Every thought I think consciously
I share with the world.

Every meal I consume consciously
I nourish and feed all beings, body and soul.

Every act of generosity I consciously engage in
I share myself with all of life.

Every conscious act of loving kindness
Loves all that is in existence.

Within every conscious act of compassion
I feel the pain and suffering of the world.

Every time I heal a part of my self
All beings heal, little by little.

Every breath I take consciously
I breathe for all of life.

There is no I
There is only All.

Remnants of abuse

A threat to survival

Abuse shapes bodies, minds, actions

Makes souls cry out in anguish

Despair fills a world with dark spaces

Hollow faces

Misplaces trust

Destroys faith in connection

Imprinted with memory

Fear flows out in cloaks of fancy dress.

The masks worn of

The powerful demon

Alive with, sometimes unintended, malice

Power equals protection

Or does the pendulum swing far

To the meek

Sublimely submitting

Fawning for safety

HEALING IS POSSIBLE

Remnants of abuse

Continued

Or both perhaps

Contextually dependent

On the drive to survive.

When safety is sincere

Hatred and fear are distilled

Into the courage of forgiveness

Trust is restored

Healing resurrects

Strengthening the compassionate will

The empowered shall rise up

And rule their own heart

Running screaming towards the light...

R U OK?

Tears this morning...
Sitting with memories of hours before
Feeling so sad for her
Most likely passed now
Running screaming towards the light
Only demons as harsh punishing company
I could feel her anguish
I could sense the cold breeze
Presence of her demons
Knowing fully they were a creation
Conjured by her confused hurt mind
Worst remnants of a horrible past
Caregivers not caring
Even dangerous
Glorified into harsh menacing monsters
Tangible in her world
Torturing her soul.

Running screaming towards the light...

Continued

She couldn't endure the maleficence
No-one should have to
Resolute for peace everlasting
She just wanted us to know...

I wish I could have held her in my arms
A buffer between her and the demons
Her last memory of compassion and presence
She deserved kindness and care
We all do.

May you feel the loving arms of the universe
Hold you close against its breast
Finding comfort in the rhythm and light
Within the beating heart of true love.
May you find Harmony in the light... RIP

Pot of gold

When we look outside ourselves

Searching for the ever elusive pot of gold

We're foolish coz

It's really the love and gratitude held in our heart,

Truth be told.

Scorpio sister

MANON

My Scorpio Sister there's something quite clear
True nature of friendship, something we both hold dear.
Not in each other's pockets but held dear in our hearts
Meet ups a challenge, but not feeling apart.
Our beautiful conversations, we converse in great depth
Exploring our hearts, the superficial never met.
You appreciate so much either simple or refined
An adventurer's spirit, delving deep in the mind.
Your friends are many with hearts open too
A sparkling reflection of the you that is true.
Your spirit is strong, your heart filled with fire
Your faith, strength, courage, and resilience I admire.
You take care of your world both inside and out
With great care for all, in that there's no doubt.
My dear Scorpio Sister, much more than a friend
No need for a label, soul sisters together without end.

Seven

CHIRON

Seven colours a rainbow makes
The simplest way to define
That's how we translate refracted light
A message to our mind.
Seven rays in planetary orbs
A solar system attunes
That's how we translate the heavenly meaning
Of planets, comets, asteroids, stars, and the moon.
Seven notes an octave tones
Music translates the language of soul
The notes of the highest octave C
Perhaps Chiron supports us to become whole.
The paradox of my poetry
Touches pain and healing felt with love
A Chironic kind of momentum
Inspiring a perspective from above.
When I only express the darkness
And the pain and hurt within
It's a sign there is work to be done
Another layer of onion peeling to begin.
Seven is a number
Revered for inner reflection
Octaves, rainbows, orbs help us attune
To universal perfection

Siblings

I miss my sister deeply
I wonder about her pain
We've fought like cats and dogs
Will I ever see you again?

The younger of my brothers
I worry about your health
I care so deeply for you
But this care is done by stealth

My eldest brother dear one
Has passed the threshold to peace
Now watching over all of us
Beyond the veil
I'm so grateful for your sweet release

I miss the ideals I hold and value
Of relationships that fill us with joy
Instead we foster conflict
All connection deemed a ploy

Something I wish you knew of me
Is the sincerity of my heart
That loves you unconditionally
Even when conflict tears us apart

Siblings

Continued

Sometimes I get where things go wrong
Sometimes confusion reigns supreme
The pieces don't make sense to me
Like an abstract nightmarish dream

I'll never turn you away
That's not a part of who I am
I'll just keep the faith and do my best
That we might become friends again

I don't always agree with things
That come across my world
But I practice deep acceptance
Knowing so much more could life unfurl

I'm OK with not knowing things
Although I would truly love to understand
Acceptance and compassion that comes from love
Graces me, as a helping hand

Simply, sorry

Hand on heart

I'm so truly sorry

For all that I know

And all that I don't

No buts...

Slow dancing with Venus backwards

You and me we changed our stride
First on, then off the merry-go-round ride
Slow dancing, our hearts took love out for a spin
We enjoyed every moment
Although contact became thin
We both had new dance cards
Where others took their turns
Necessary things that we had to both do
With great challenges and lessons still to learn
Just look where we are now
Slow dancing together again today
Good friends and dear lovers
Together, we live laugh and play
We've shared deep respect and kindness
All the way through
Our journey of friendship and love
And all that feels true
Moment by moment
We explore our new start
Passion still blooming
We come from the heart
Venus in reverse
Might not bode too well
Unless lessons are learned
And themes are felled

Solidarity sister

JOANNE

We have friends in high places
That brought us together
Our spirits aim high
Like birds of a Feather
I treasure our dailies
Sweet hellos or great text chats
We cover some ground with some days
A bright mood, and some days are flat
No matter which one
We make time anyway
To connect from our hearts
To brighten each day
Bragatoire tales brighten our days
With gifs and shared laughter
We work our way through the maze
Of Challenges in body
And mind giving us gyp
We muddle on daily
Sore hands, feet, or hip
We research together
Seeking ways to move through
With healthy solutions
From medicine, and food too
We lift each other up

Solidarity sister

Continued

With stories to cope
And healing with Spirit
Enlivening great hope
For days of more comfort
To walk, laugh, or run
We uncover some joy
In friendship connection and fun
Daily we chat or
At least, check in and say "hi"
Or speak of dreams or philosophy
Or tales of the day just gone by
Your good man beside you
Who often says hi
Just adds to the treasure of friendship
As the days go by.
Our hearts have in common
Many values and align
With care and connection
Most definitely a good sign
Of friendship we value
A trusting of care
Our dailies inform us
That solidarity is there.

Spirit of a healing flower

CHRISSIE

The Tuberose is beautiful beyond verbal description
Unaware of its own presence, and its beauty's encryption
It grows and blossoms without any care
Not knowing how others believe or, in wonder, stare
Its presence delight all senses and feeling
Unaware of its gift of joy, beauty, and healing
Tuberose just does what's innate and knows best
It grows as itself, for others a true bequest
I see this in you, a gift to all beings
A gift of beauty, of presence, of healing with meaning
Keep blossoming your truth in your own unique way
Bringing joy, comfort, and healing to all every day
Reiki, yoga, and All Love, your masterful flow
A gift to us all, I think you should know
Don't stop to think about your way of being
Just keep shining your light with your own truth and leaning
I treasure your daily "good mornings" with blessings and meaning
Each day you share love in your way, leaving your world beaming.

Such a pain!

SELF-CARE

My body hurts
It's such a pain
I've had enough
Of this refrain
So out of tune
With sweet soft notes
It simply hurts
No help from quotes
Inevitable pain
Suffering again
The most likely option
Causing me
Inner commotion
Even though this pain
Sparks up emotion
Just keep going
Plodding along
Breathe in breathe out
With focus strong
Feel kindness and care
And loves sweet song.
Thank you body
You're doing your best
Time to honour you
Time to rest

Sun shower

JOY IN PRESENCE

The sunlight beaming through the clouds
Raindrops are falling
Tapping like the rhythm of the world's soul
It's beating heart gently tapping on leaves, tin rooves
All things glistening in the sunlight
Droplets like jewels, diamonds galore
Reflecting a million facets and rainbows
Tiny in each bubble of joy.
Flowers are smiling
Leaves are dancing
Face is beaming with delight at the sound of tapping
Moist air on skin
Clear water droplets on the tongue
Poking out in joy to sample the freshness
The scent of damp air and wet grass
And this wondrous shimmering sight
All senses alive and in love
Water straight from heaven
Simply... a sun shower.

Taking it all in

PRESENCE

How do the blossoms that we see grow

Into the fruit that we know

The waves that flow onto the sand

Reaching here from another land

The cottonwool clouds up in the sky

All changing form as they float by

Sounds of waves, birds, and engines keen

All present even though some, sight unseen

The taste of water crystal clear

And all the senses we hold dear

The brilliant sun warm on my skin

I wonder where this all begins

It's all connected in time and space

Taking it all in

Continued

I'm sensing here now in this one place

The people places and all the things

That touch our lives with thoughts they bring

There is no time and space you see

All things are one, a part of me

I am them, and you are me

The rock, the litter, the bird, and tree

And so respect it all I do

The all, the one, the me, and you

The mystery of this life unfolds

In precious moments for us to hold

Writing this just makes me smile

Connecting me with what's worthwhile

Tears of remorse

SIMPLY, SORRY

Shedding tears now
For all the pain I've caused
Wishing that I had taken time
Had known enough to pause
I tried so hard consciously
History to not repeat
Instead making things worse
Unconsciously sinking slowly into defeat
My heart and mind remorseful
Proof is in the pudding now
Children long angry and astray
And not loving me somehow
I wish we'd find the way back home
I wish our hearts could mend
I wish unconditional love could prevail
And we'd become a family again.

The wetlands

Paperbarks line winding paths
Chirping birds flitting around vines of hearts
Moths, butterflies and stingless bees
Honey makers, nature's keepers of nectar in the trees
Traffic noise intrudes from over there
Close by there is peace so I don't care
Colours vivid all shades and hues
Nature's palette masters magnificent views
Pig face hiding among the grass
A home for insects that humans bypass
Mozzies bloodthirsty come to rest
Challenging my stillness, I'm put to the test
So moving on before I'm eaten alive
This beautiful wetland will continue to thrive
Sheoaks dappling afternoon light
The boardwalk path winding out of sight
Lovers strolling walk hand in hand
Kissed by dappled light along the path of sand
Salt and sweet the waters flow
Creating natures wetlands perfectly just so.

The writing's on the wall

Word art
Colourful words
Sparkling with promise
Adjectives describe
My dream for me
Nouns place facts
Verbs, my actions
Pronouns my people
All of my dreams
Or at least
Those I can name
Words are my images
They tell my story
Of life's sweet dreams
Of my future
In all their glory

Love
Joy
Counselling
Good Nutrition
Star Gazing
My Beautiful Home.
Coffee
Bushwalking
Music
Books
Freedom
Enjoy Food
Nature
Culture
Comfort
Warm Welcome
Friendships
Satisfied Clients
Magic
Grandchildren
Playing
Trust
Children
Connection
Respect
Family
Fun
Publishing
Community
Metaphysics
Abundance
Paddling
Meditation
Sharing
Reading
Linen and Silk
Gardens
Care
Space
Reiki
Harmony
Walking
Compassion
Psychotherapy
Nourishing
Hugs
Life

Thomas Conor

MY BEAUTIFUL SON - YOU TOOK MY BREATH AWAY

Our delightful Irish boy
Now a strong and handsome man
I'm celebrating your life in words
To me you are truly "grand"

A blessing to our lives
In '91, you were one of three
You chose to see it through
In '92, the one who came to be

Avocados were our pleasure
With Raspberry vinegar filled to the brim
And then I discovered Lion bars
The dentist found my cravings grim

Those delightful little pleasures
Just added to the joy
Of the wonder of you growing inside me
Into my gorgeous baby boy

Thomas Conor

Continued

Around 2 am you woke me
On Bastille Day '92
By 6.30 that morning
I held you in my arms
My love for you so true

Your sister came to greet you
A gift offered in her tiny hands
Her joy to finally meet you
And awe, as she held you in her arms

Your big sister loved you to pieces
Her dear sweet baby bro
Our dear family now equalled four
I watched your dad's heart glow

Your first year spent in Dublin
And travelled half way round the world
Your smile and gentle nature
All could see beginning to unfurl

One day you struggled breathing
Just couldn't catch your breath
I slept under your hospital bed that night
My dear son to protect

At one year old we took you homeward
To become an Aussie lad
The Irish peat smog and firesides
For your young lungs were bad

You grew and thrived and got so tall
And towered over me in fun
 Saying "Don't make me come down there and say that"
Your wonderful sense of humour had my heart won

I know there's been some sad times
Regrets and great "to do"
There are so many beautiful memories
Of days spent in joy with you

Thomas Conor

Continued

So many a cherished memory
One dearly comes to mind
The veggie platter served to me, breakfast in bed
Orange and peanut butter juice made by your own hand

I delighted in each mouthful
Could taste the love and fun in there
In the food and drink created
For your mum with intent and care

We climbed a mountain together one day
Through the night to see the dawn
The day began with clouds and mist
But at the summit
The atmosphere was warm

I struggled to descend the mountain walk
Shuffling for hours step by step
You stayed beside me all the way
Cheering me on
My hero, my side you never left

We'd spend weekends baking biscuits and bread
Your dad had you and Em cook at home too
It seems something in these moments touched you
And cooking became part of you

We saw you struggle as teens can do
And then you found your way
This delightful baker came to life
Up so early every day

Then you found another path
Following Grandfather's naval ways
From then you sailed the seven seas
Nourishing mates throughout your day

Dear Grandfather is sailing with you
The gypsy told me so
He's there to protect and guide you
Just thought I'd let you know

Thomas Conor

Continued

I love the way you nourish souls
I've seen the smile upon your face
I hope you always feel great love
For however you fill your time and space

I'm hoping that you're happy
Satisfied in all you do
I hope you find a sweet, sweet love
As wonderful as you

My wish for you always my son
No matter where your heart leads
That you know how I so love you, and
Always wishing you "fair winds and following seas".

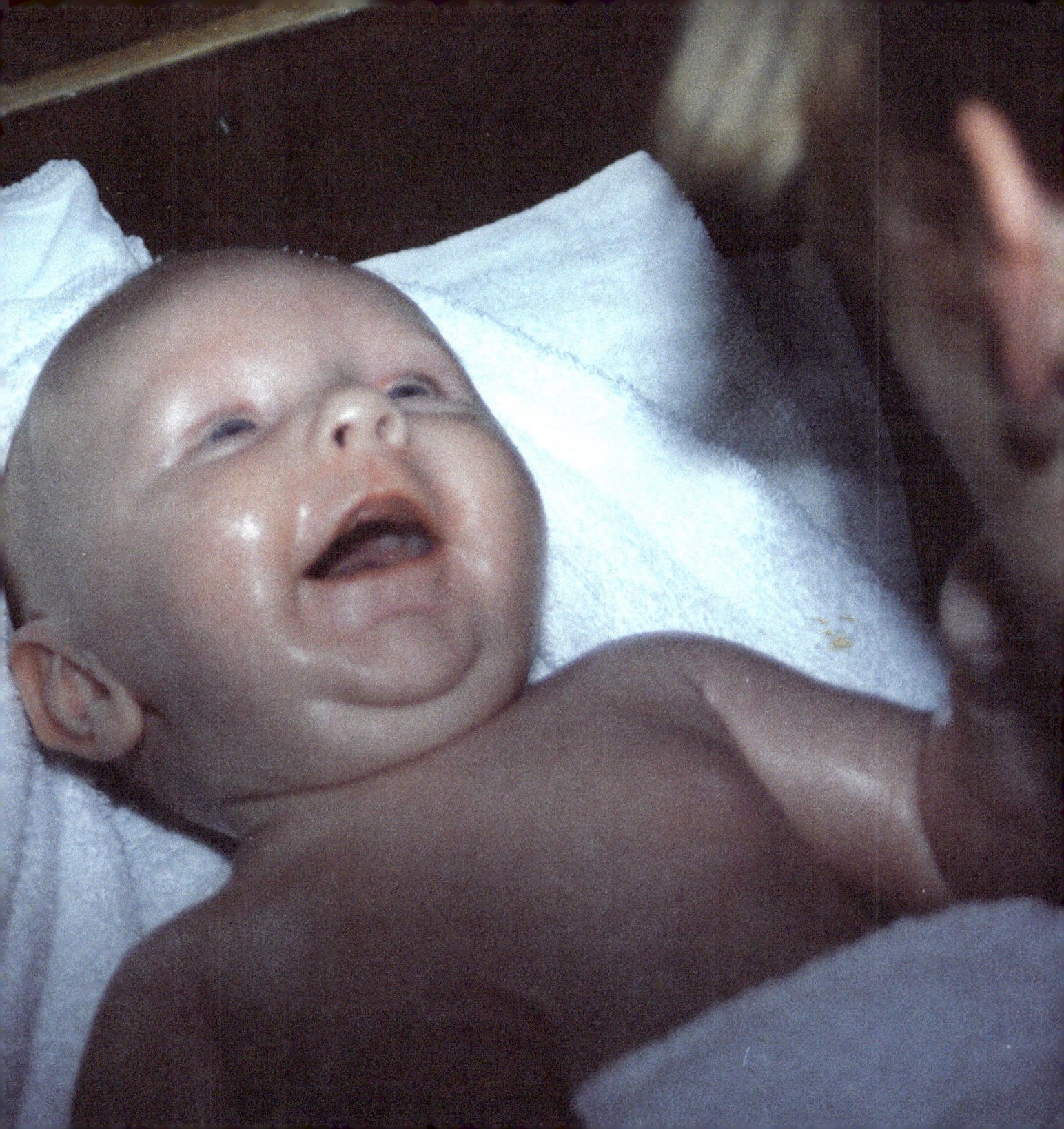

Two years

FOR WAYNE 27TH AUG 1955 - 21ST MAR 2019

I said as I kissed your forehead
"See you later, I'll be back in tomorrow"
As if I didn't know that
Seeing Jesus at your bedside
Denial that you would go
Foretold of all our sorrow.

I'm grateful for the time together
In the last months of your life
Too much precious time spent apart for years
Fear, anger unforgiving, all distancing
Amongst the usual family strife.

I left your bedside that afternoon
Headed for a favourite beachside spot
Searching for some peace of mind
A breathing space
To untie a tight, heartfelt, inner knot.

Two years

Continued

The ocean and the trees
I'm always enamoured by the view
Captured a most unusual sky
And cloudbursts that day
I wondered later if that was you.

Preparing for your final road home
To leave this earthly plane
Headed for those green pastures
To lay your weary body down,
Our lives would never be the same.

The sky darkened, clouds playing innocently
Sun setting over mountains to the west
The east akin to the valley of the shadow of death
Illuminated now, an unusual Equinox full moon rise with
Ascending Virgo beckoning you to rest.

Two years

Continued

Your Virgo angel rising with the brightest of moons
Guiding you through the night
Leading you over the still moonlit ocean waters
I whispered to her "today is a good day to die..."
Jesus still loyal by your side
As you transcended into the light.

I'm so grateful you held good company
Your own prayers answered to guide you through
As I remember you with love today
This anniversary number two.

Unlimited friendliness

INSPIRED BY PEMA CHÖDRÖN

Don't mistake my friendliness for something more than joy
When you make much more of it, friendship becomes a ploy
None of us is special, equal souls on a unique path
All trying to make it home to the warmth of loves welcome hearth
Don't mistake my friendliness I'm not your little toy
I'm just trying to be your inspiration, your sense of hope and joy
I'm no-one's toy to play with, and cast aside when bored
We could break each other's hearts, of that you can rest assured
So let me be myself, to laugh, and simply be your friend
To share the joy of life, without in mind another end
Friendships can be filled with love, no gender bias there
Just free spirits enjoying life, with true love, compassion, and care
So don't mistake my friendship, my laughter and attention is not a flirt
Just simply enjoying who you are, I appreciate your worth
I aim to see the best in you and help you see it too
But don't mistake my friendship as some great forever ado
Since childhood my whole fantasy has had a simple theme
Wanting all to love themselves has been my favourite meme

Unlimited friendliness

Continued

So many times along my path dark nightmares have sprung forth
From this simple dream of love for all, I lost my own self-worth
Sometimes I would become confused mistaking what was true
Mistaking what true love really means and how to see it through
I don't believe in besties, too much pressure on each one
To live up to expectations, no equanimity and no fun
So don't mistake my friendliness or what true love means to me
Always a wish to see us all achieve our greatest dreams
A reason, season, a lifetime, we cannot really know
The purpose of a friendship as people come and go
I'll do my best to love you in my own clumsy unique way
But don't mistake my friendliness and lead us to the fray
My intention is to show you your own soul's light and heart
Not an opening for meanness, or for you to tear me apart
Don't mistake my friendliness, you're all my special muse
Me giving from my heart is not something you can misuse
Don't mistake my friendliness, I've learned boundaries from day to day
I accept your way of being, you are here to find your own way

Sometimes the need to retreat to show myself some care
I express to you as best I can that I know you are there
But don't mistake my friendship at the times I do retreat
My heart is always with you, I'm not an enemy to defeat
I don't always know how to be there, as you might expect
But don't mistake my friendliness, or the way I send my texts
Let's try to balance give and take – it happens anyway
I'll check with you if I have doubt, I'll ask if you're OK
Don't mistake my friendliness, it's filled with love and faith
In you making your own journey, to work through your own mistakes
I accept your choice and boundaries even when not what I would say
I won't mistake your friendship, not liking me is totally OK
You don't have to love me, you don't have to approve
The mere fact that you exist, towards you my heart will move
So let's not mistake this friendliness that comes from the heart
Let's be the best that we can be, forgive and make a new start
I don't always get things right, sometimes my head gets in the way
My heart just knows that love exists, and I love you anyway.

Walking in the rain

You took my breath away

PRESENCE

You took my breath away today
Senses alive here and there
The grey sea and sky
Shades through mist
Foam of the waves tinged with beige
An egret sheltering
Breast feathers caught by the breeze
Floating softly to and fro
Perhaps in tune with its beating heart.

You took my breath away today
Stinging water
Like pinpricks of joy
On my cheek
Rain heading to land
Across the water
Smelling and tasting the ocean
Inhaled in each breath.

Walking in the rain

Continued

You took my breath away today
Bursts of bitter-sweetness arrest my taste buds
The Brazilian cherries glossy red frilliness
Glistening in delight
With droplets of spring rain
Disguising the moist flesh
Sharing the delicious joy with birds and ants
I feel the healing and gratitude
Unaware of the sacred geometry
In the leaves
The flowers
And yes
In the constructions of humankind.

You took my breath away today
Feeling raindrops
Run like tears
In between my breasts
Awakening my heart

An extension of all beings
Feeling the pain of dear souls
Spiralling into bitterness
Anger
Grief
Fear...
How to heal
How to share the beauty of life
The sights of stormy skies
Sounds of the wind, waves, and birds
The oh so sweet scent of nectar and salt
The delightful taste of blossoms that self-actualized
The gentle kiss of a rain shower
As the universe wholeheartedly greets me.

You took my breath away today
Opened my eyes
My mind
My heart

Walking in the rain

Continued

My senses
Coloured my world with beauty.

I wish with all my heart I knew
How to take someone's breath away
Soothe and soften aching souls
Lift dampened spirits
But, thank you...
For today
Again
You took my breath away...

War of worlds

THE SHADOW

To their face, your words sweetly tell them yes
Your actions betray the words and speak of no
Gaslighting is such a hurtful power play
Undermining, a painful way to flow
The knives in peoples backs
Silently and subtly stab through hearts
As you manipulate the world
Playing your differential parts
We all manipulate our world in some way
As we meet our individual needs
Survival is the key there
Driving intention, survival always leads
I wonder of your intention for
The good of others or yourself
It's as if your good intentions
Have been left upon the shelf
I'm wondering what your heart needs
To stop these dreadful power plays

War of worlds

Continued

Inside you must be hurting badly
Survival needs, eating through your days
Stop making other people wrong
To puff you up with pride
One day without self-recognition
Your behaviour will cause your downward slide
You know, we could work together
With the objective of pure love
To serve for joy of others
An olive branch on the wings of the white dove
But my idealism doesn't serve me well
Dreams of peace interrupt my sleep
As I understand our human nature
And how survival needs will always run deep
Let's end this war between us now
I am not your enemy, you are not my foe
Let in the light to shine on us both
To allow peace and love to grow.

What am I doing?

SEEKING DIRECTION

What am I doing here
Frozen in time
My connection to spirit
Much less than sublime
I'm lost...
No direction....
That feels true to my heart
Just marking time now
Til it's time to depart.
Thinking of children
A wish for their joy
Just love and connection,
No attachment, or ploy
The direction I take now
Is all up to me
My love and my happiness
Is my responsibility
I want to let go
Give it all up to God
I just don't know how yet
So onward daily, I plod...

What if...

RAINBOWS

What if the sky was blue
And if the grass was green
Could we better lift our hearts
Beyond moon and stars
To places unseen
What if sunflowers were yellow
Or even the brightest gold
Could we sing 'til our hearts felt mellow
Until we just grew old
What if the grass was green
What if the sky was blue
Could I keep you safe in my heart
Forever me and you.
What if blood was red
And we could bleed to death
Would we leave things unsaid
Unloved beyond last breath.
What if life was a rainbow
A broken ray of light
Heaven sent to show us
That everything's alright...

Where soul meets spirit

HEART SPACE

It's the soul that aches and cries out in pain

It's the spirit that heals like a cleansing rain

It's the heart that sees both with loving eyes

Holding the middle space with love

And truth without guise

Hold your soul's journey and miraculous path

With the transcendence of spirit

So they can meet in your earthly heart.

Why

A BIGGER VIEW

Everyone is our teacher we can't pick and choose
If the lessons reflected are not recognised
Peace and harmony, the student will likely lose.
Some teachers we carefully seek out
To teach us how to consciously grow
In the hope that their wisdom and way of being
Awakens us gently to all we need to know.

The teachers we resist the most are also love in action
Showing shadow sides of ourselves
Often in unconscious retraction.
An evolutionary process is wise to recognise
As we peel away layers of the onion
Carefully raising self-awareness
Including all that we disown and despise.

Our partners can be our biggest challenge
They start out as "hail fellow well met"
And as time goes on
With familiarity and unawareness
They can become our deepest regret.

Why

Continued

Our job is to understand ourselves
Bring our open-heart and self-compassion to the fore.
If we can learn to love all parts of us
We could love our partners even more.

Our families are the tribe we choose way before our birth
Our greatest teachers that life can give
From love to anger, grief to mirth.
Our family's role is to reflect to us our foibles and our blessings
To show us our true inner self
And all the stuff, seen and not
That we're most definitely expressing.

Practice makes it perfectly held with respect, gratitude, and grace
Keep it all in balance, being centred and aware
Keep coming back to hand on heart
Put that softened smile upon your face
Back to love, kindness, presence, and care.

Wishing for peace

PANDEMICS POLITICS POWERMONGERS

I wish, I wish, I wish

The world would just fade away

Too many angry people

With too many games to play

Opinions closing minds

With way too much to say

Why can't we just love each other

And say that from the heart

Instead of spewing hatred

That tear our lives apart

I feel anger rise within me

I know I'm not immune

I pray for love and guidance

So I may sing a different tune.

Amen

Wired to survive

HEART-MIND

We are wired for self help

Imperative one learns to understand

In each a deep inner well

Dip the cup deeply

Raising wisdom to the surface

A natural development process

Growth towards light like a beautiful flowering garden

Sometimes delayed from too much shade

Watering the weeds of a life out of balance

Not the seeds that nourish the soul

Instead unnecessary seeds of flowering fear

Driving survival out of balance

Out of its natural place.

But we bring wisdom with us

A connection between consciousness, brain, and nerves

Inherent and hidden beyond neural pathways

Immeasurable, intangible

Intuition is the raw talent

Synchronicity abounds for the mindful

Interpretation dictates the result

Clouded lenses filter the senses

Perceptions congregating in the mind.

Listen well my friend

Open the eyes, blink, and blink again

Feel the tingling shiver rise through your whole being

All senses alive

Develop wisely so that perceptions congregate

In the neural pathways of your heart

WTF?!?!

WHY THE FACE?

WTF?
What's going on?
Why the mood so dark?
Why are tears flowing?
Why this deep heaviness of heart?

WTF?
Just matching the weather
Dark stormy skies
Ferocious wind blowing
Raindrops stinging sad eyes

WTF?
Feelings overflowing
Thoughts running too deep
This too shall pass
Your confidence I'll keep

WTF?
So, why the face?
I care, it's ok
Let's walk side by side
And like a Phoenix,
You'll rise again today.

Wyzdom

Is it wyze

To analyze

Or take a leap of faith?

The mind paralyzed

And hypnotyzed

Not knowing it's true place.

Are you polaryzed

And your life dramatyzed

Your world swinging to and fro?

Time to centralyze

And normalyze

An open heart allows wyzdom to flow.

Grandmotherhood

I am so grateful to allow the tears to flow

A stream of beauty shaping the landscape of hills and valleys of a rich life

Watering the seeds of the most exquisite coloured wildflowers of loving thoughts

Poignant joy blossoming into life

New blooms flourishing with each rising sun

A new generation of the magnificent harvest of the seed of my dreams

Children a blessing, a gift

A seed to be nurtured in the garden of life

A continuation of love...

Milo William

WITH LOVE FROM GRAN

Welcome beautiful boy!

My heart wants to wrap you in a warm blanket of love.

May you always feel loved

May you always feel safe

May you always know in your heart

Of your divine place

In a world that is harsh

And beautifully raw

Filled with lessons and laughter

May you always have more

Joy and good health

Dear friends who align

With the purest of hearts

Milo William

Continued

And a great ethical incline

May you be supported and protected

Enough that you thrive

So your heart may grow strong

And you walk with gentleness in your stride

May you always have faith

That people are innately good

And when life challenges this with hardship

May you lean on solid brotherhood

May your village always stand by you

Share your sorrows and joy

May your life be meaningful for you always

My dear grandchild Milo, a beautiful boy.

POWER OF PRAYER

A prayer for healing

The world is in turmoil in so many ways.
I'm feeling the need for attention on intention
Of healing people, the planet, all things living as each new day dawns
One and all deserving an honourable mention.
Meditation, prayer: it doesn't matter how
Just bring a heartfelt intention to the here and the now.
Candles lit with a word to the light
Asking for guidance on how this prayer of love and healing
Might be powerful, spread out infinitely, and be right.
Each person unique and collectively I acknowledge and mention
Lighting some candles to start the intention ball rolling
My roll call in mind of suffering, my mind starts scrolling.
My mind whispers your name as my hand stays tenderly on my heart
I wish for all healing and that you feel ready to do your part.
Sensing so many open hearts across the world too
Synchronistically meditating, praying from their own world view.
I rejoice in this time for presence, all I need is within me
This attention on intention, I feel the smile on my face
For healing and love, in this sacred space.

Footprints in my heart

All size and shaped feet have walked through my life

Tiptoed, stomped, tickled, and kicked as sharp as a knife

Each footprint a memory divine in its presence

Marking my heart and defining my essence

Work of art or a wound, a tattoo or a scar

Each impression has touched me from near or from far

Nothing is forgotten, it's all captured in there

Exposed in my soul and emotions laid bare

I know that more footprints will walk into my heart

To endure or enliven, coloured 'til death us do part

Each footprint a diamond, precious gems I've gained

That renders my soul forever changed.

May I learn to tiptoe gently
When I enter your heart

I wish that I could take your breath away in Love...

I am grateful